Windjammers Downeast

by

Fred LeBlanc

WoodenBoat BOOKS
BROOKLIN, MAINE USA

Published by
WoodenBoat Books
Naskeag Road, PO Box 78
Brooklin, Maine 04616 USA
www.woodenboatbooks.com

ISBN 10: 1-934982-00-8
ISBN 13: 978-1-934982-00-6

First Printing 2009

Front Cover: The schooner HERITAGE
Back Cover: Schooners AMERICAN EAGLE, NATHANIEL BOWDITCH, and STEPHEN TABER

All images by Frederick LeBlanc, except back cover author photo, by Claire LeBlanc.

Book design: BasRelief Design

Printed in U.S.A. by Taylor Publishing

10 9 8 7 6 5 4 3 2 1

Cruising among the three thousand wild and unspoiled islands dotting the coast of Maine, considered to be one of the most beautiful sailing destinations in the world, are the last of a great fleet of windjammers. Many of them transported cargoes of raw materials and supplies along the eastern seaboard; some fished the Grand Banks, and others were originally built as private yachts. Several have been designated National Historic Landmarks. These restored vessels, along with re-creations of the past now host passengers on adventure cruises. The Maine windjammer fleet provides a unique opportunity to escape to another era and experience a time when sailing vessels ruled the sea, as they did a hundred years ago, using only seamanship and canvas to harness the power of the wind and sea.

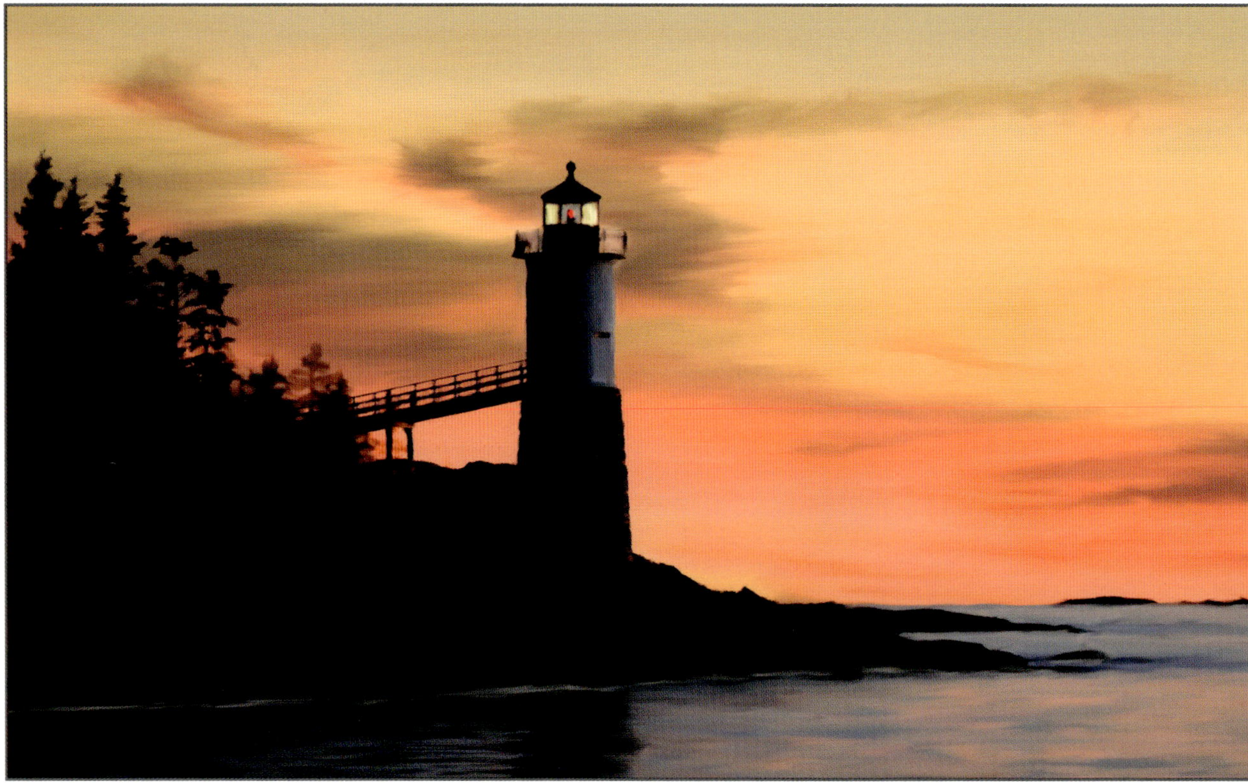

Robinson Point Light

CONTENTS

AMERICAN EAGLE

Built in 1930 by the United Sail Loft Co., for Captain Patrick Murphy and launched as ANDREW & ROSALIE, she was renamed AMERICAN EAGLE in 1941. She was the last auxiliary schooner built in Gloucester, Massachusetts, and she is the oldest known Gloucester power and sailing fishing schooner afloat. In 1986 after 55 years of fishing, she was rebuilt for the windjammer passenger trade. Based in Rockland, Maine, she is owned and operated by Captain John Foss.

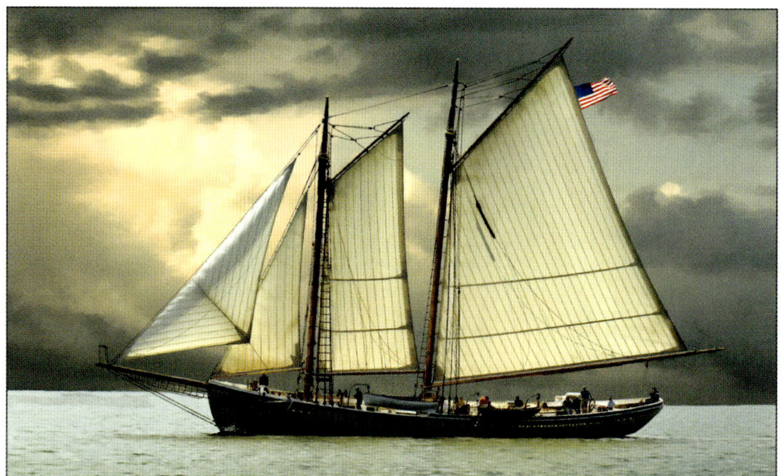

Length on Deck: 92′
Length Over All: 125′
Beam: 20′
Draft: 11′ 4″
Displacement: 107 tons
Sail Area: 4600 sq. feet
Rig: bald-headed schooner
Power: 109hp diesel
Passengers: 26
Crew: 5

www.schooneramericaneagle.com

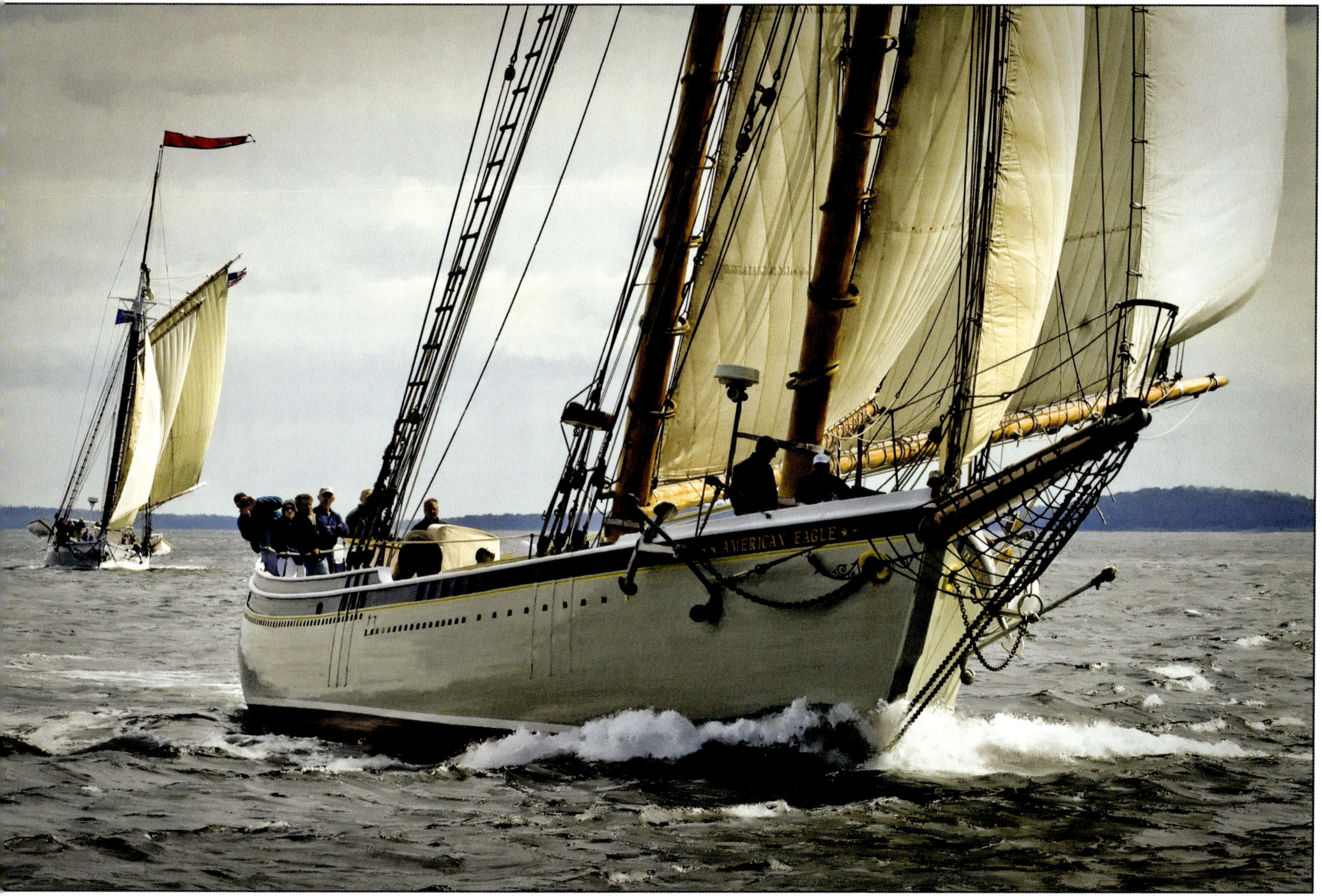
AMERICAN EAGLE

ANGELIQUE

Built in Florida in 1981 for the Maine windjammer passenger trade, ANGELIQUE was designed by Camden, Maine artist Imero Gobbato, and is based on British Brixham fishing trawlers of the 1880s. ANGELIQUE is the only steel-hulled windjammer in the Maine fleet. Owned and operated by Captain Mike & Lynn McHenry, she hails from Camden, Maine.

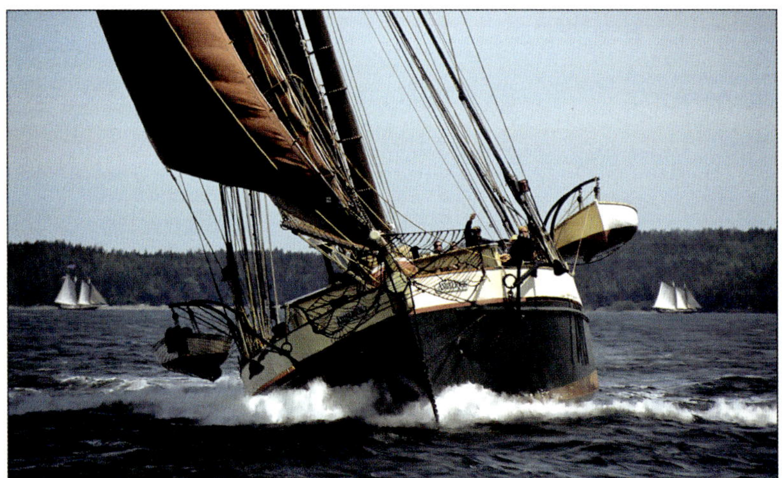

Length On Deck: 95′
Length Over All: 130′
Beam: 23′ 7″
Draft: 11′ 6″
Displacement: 142 tons
Sail Area: 5269 sq. feet
Rig: gaff topsail ketch
Power: two 471 Detroit diesels
Passengers: 31
Crew: 7

www.sailangelique.com

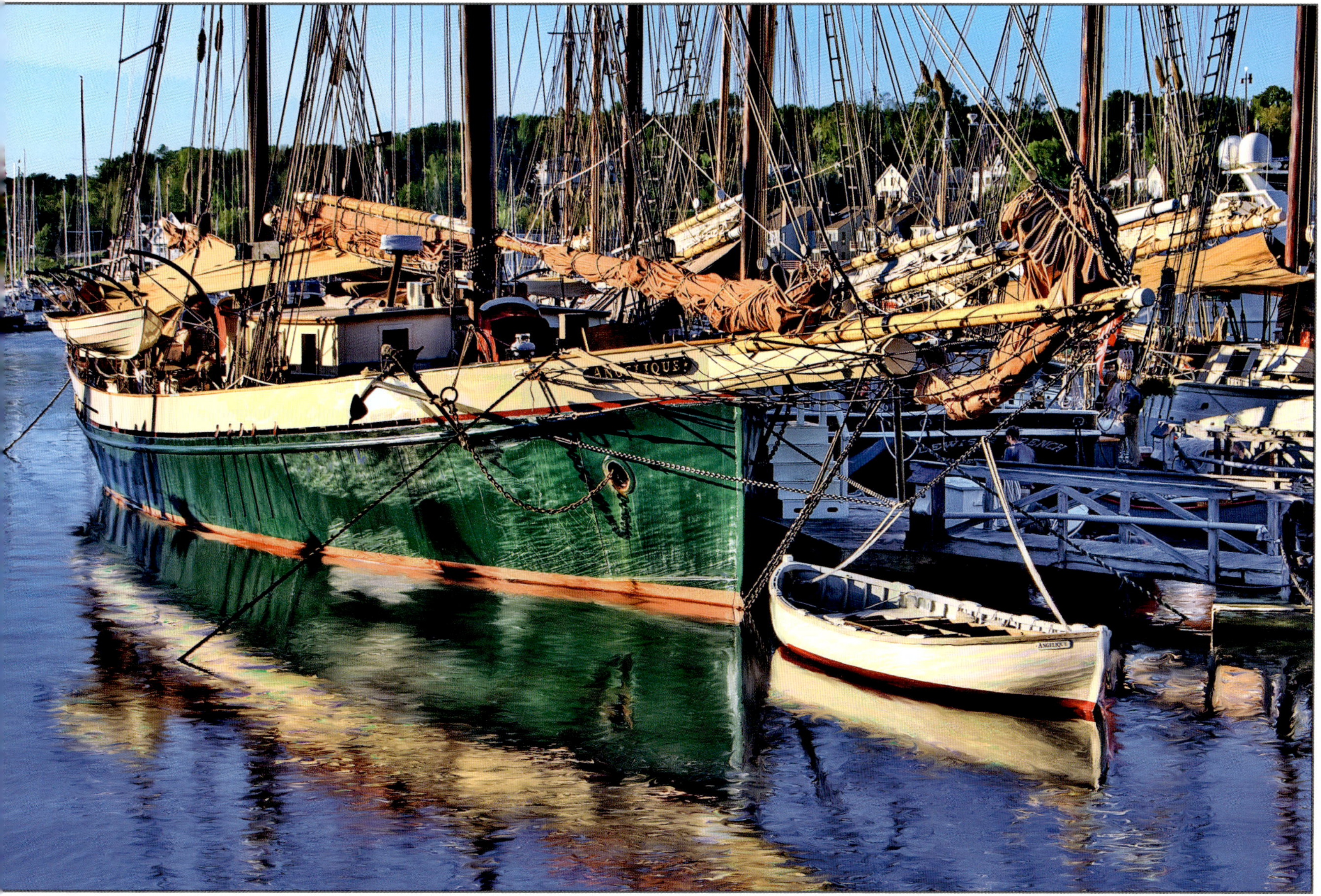

GRACE BAILEY

GRACE BAILEY was built in Patchogue, Long Island, New York, in 1882 by Oliver Perry Smith. Considered the freight trucks of their time, she carried hard pine wood from Georgia and the Carolinas to New York. During the winter months she sailed to the West Indies for the fruit trade. In 1939 she became one of the first windjammers to carry vacationing passengers along the coast of Maine, and she is now a National Historic Landmark. Owned and operated since 1986 by Captain Ray Williamson, her home port is Camden, Maine.

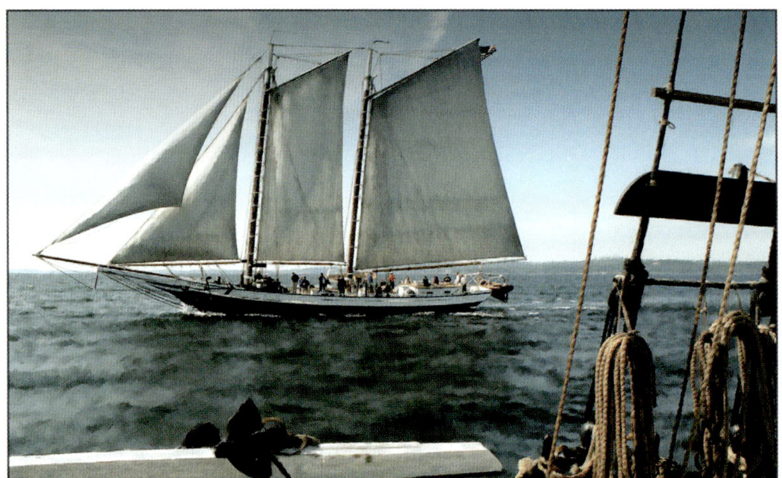

Length on Deck: 81′
Length Over All: 123′
Beam: 23′ 6″
Draft: 7′ (11′ 6′ centerboard down)
Displacement: 59 tons
Sail Area: 3985 sq. feet
Rig: bald-headed schooner
Power: yawl boat
Passengers: 29
Crew: 5

www.mainewindjammercruises.com

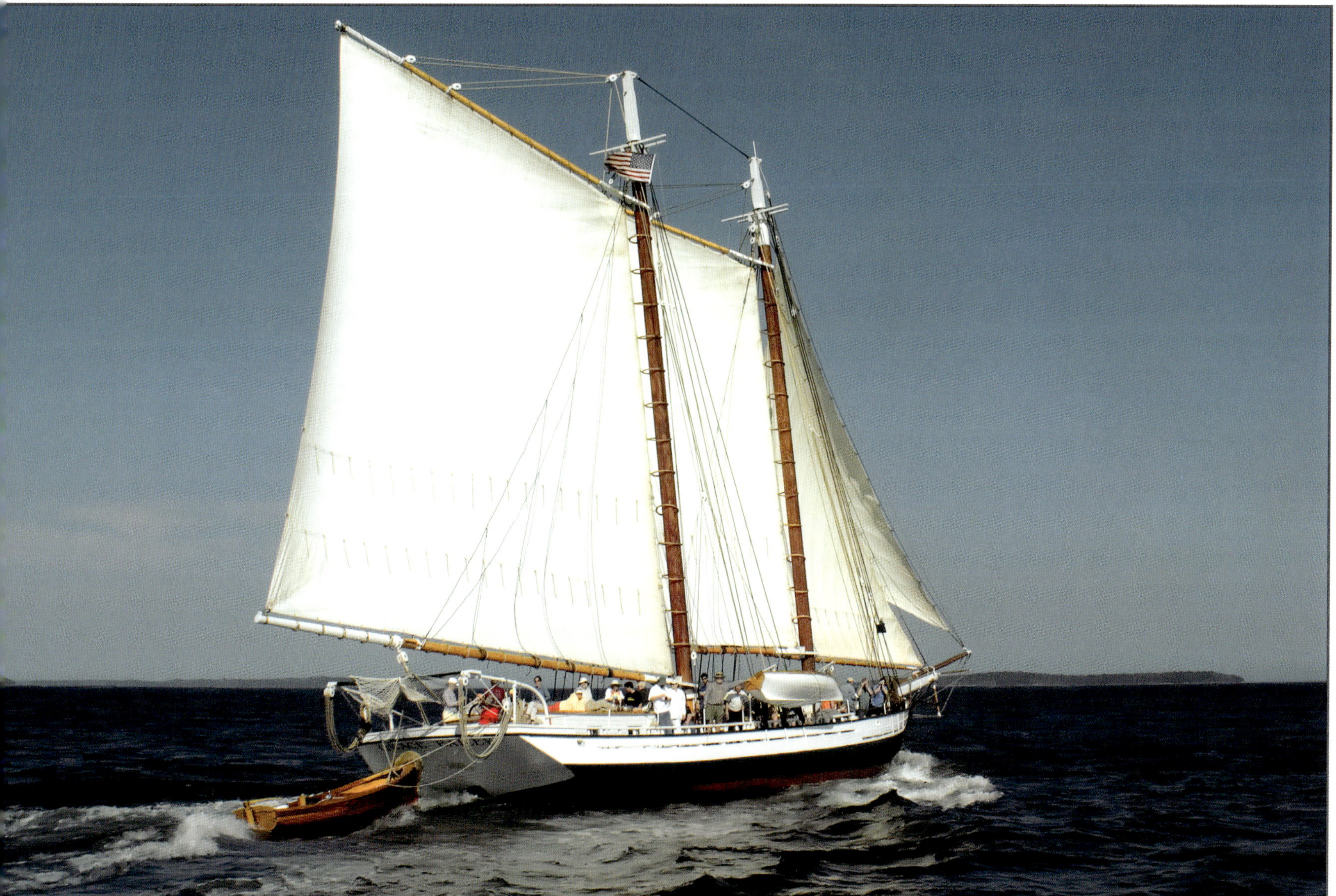

HERITAGE

HERITAGE was launched on April 16, 1983 at the historic North End Shipyard in Rockland, Maine. Built, designed, owned, and operated by Captains Doug and Linda Lee, HERITAGE was designed in the tradition of the 19th century coasters and is powered only by a yawl boat. She carries an original 1917 one-lunger donkey engine to raise the anchor and hoist the sails. The Lee's interest in the maritime history of Maine has been the foundation of the HERITAGE's design. She is not a replica, but rather the next generation of coasting schooner, designed specifically with comfort and safety in mind. She hails from Rockland, Maine.

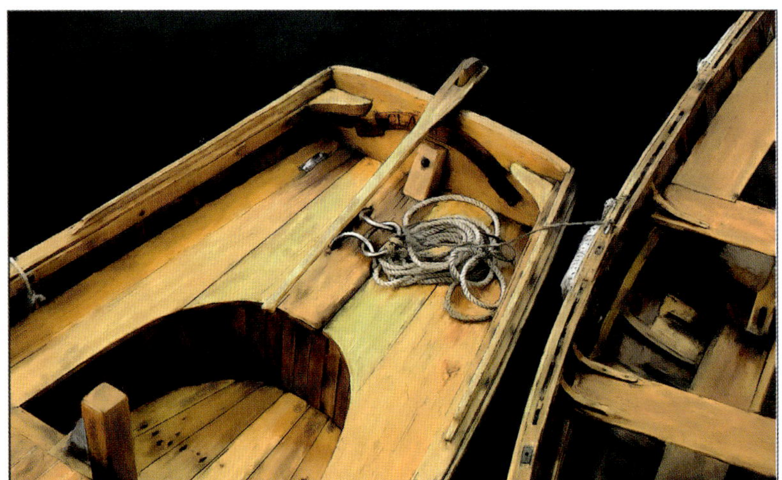

Length on Deck: 95′
Length Over All: 145′
Beam: 24′
Draft: 8′ (18′ centerboard down)
Displacement: 153 tons
Sail Area: 5200 sq. feet
Rig: main topsail schooner
Power: yawl boat
Passengers: 33
Crew: 6

www.schoonerheritage.com

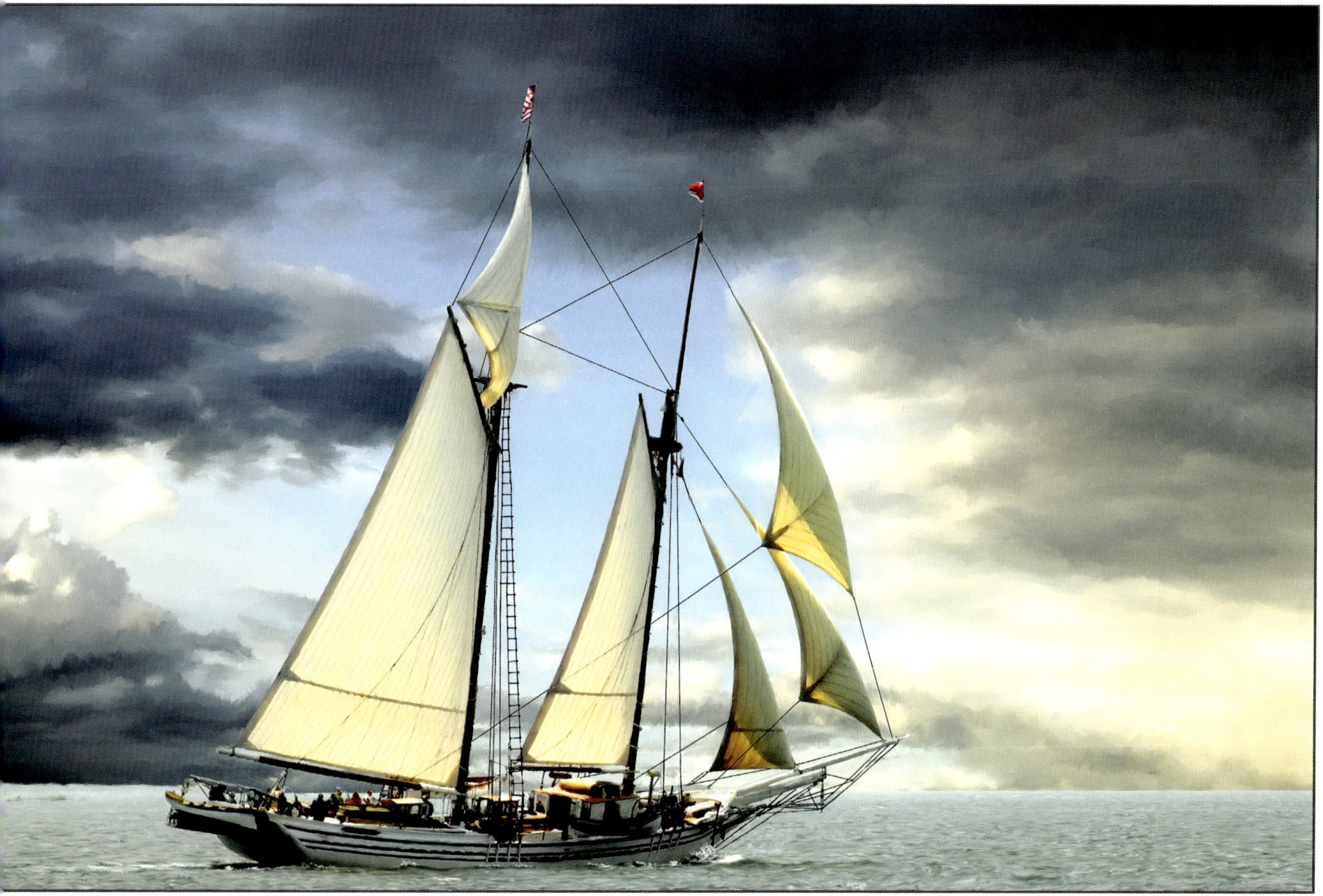

ISSAC H. EVANS

The ISSAC H. EVANS was built in 1886 by George Vannaman in Mauricetown, New Jersey, as an oyster fisherman on Delaware Bay. She has since been designated a National Historic Landmark representing the 19th century Delaware Bay oystermen. In 1971 she was brought "Downeast" and completely rebuilt by Percy and Small Shipyard for the Maine windjammer passenger trade. Today she is berthed at the North End Shipyard in Rockland, and is owned and operated by Captain Brenda Thomas.

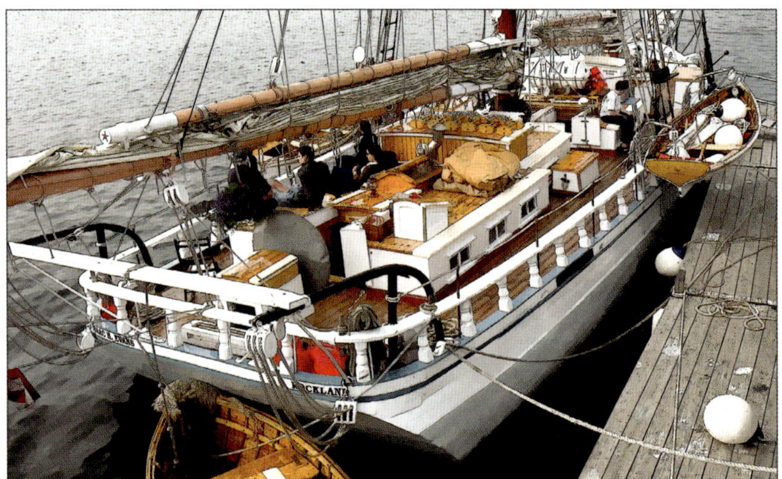

Length on Deck: 65′
Length Over All: 99′
Beam: 19′
Draft: 6′ (13′ centerboard down)
Sail Area: 2600 sq. feet
Displacement: 68 tons
Rig: main topsail schooner
Power: yawl boat
Passengers: 22
Crew: 4

www.midcoast.com/~evans

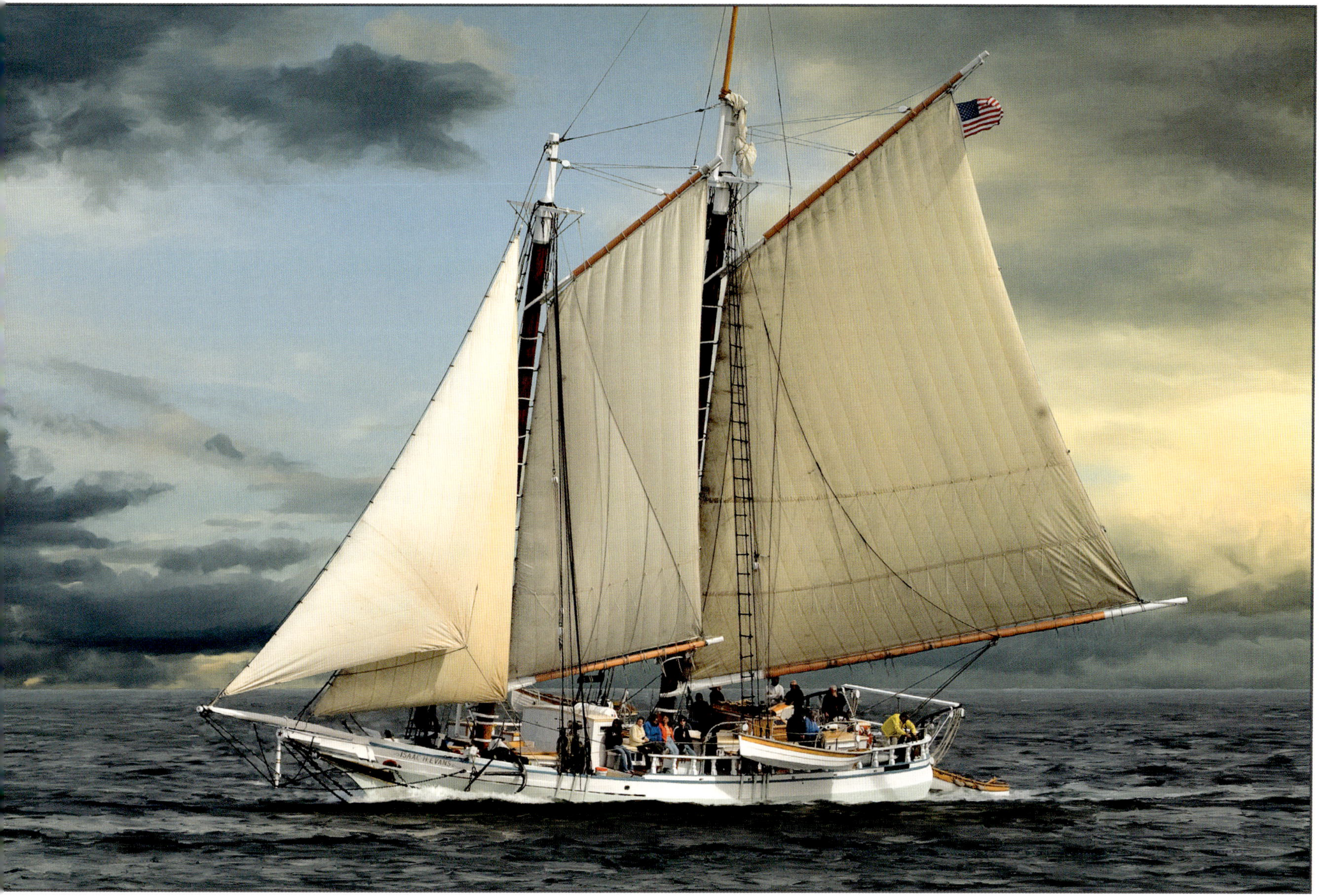
ISAAC H. EVANS

J.&E. RIGGIN

The J.&E. RIGGIN was built in 1927 in Dorchester, New Jersey, for oyster dredging on Delaware Bay. She was converted in 1940 to power, and began ground and mackerel fishing in Cape Cod Bay and Long Island Sound. In the early 1970s the engine was removed and cabins were added for the passenger trade. Today she is owned and operated by Captains Jon Finger and Anne Mahle, and sails out of Rockland, Maine.

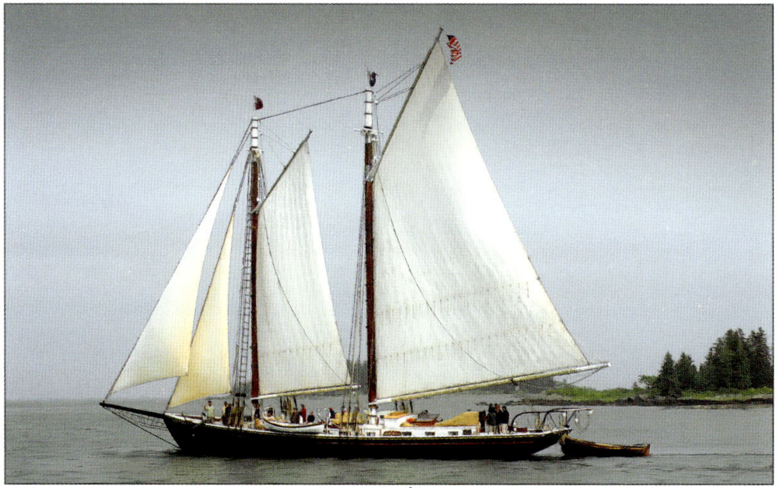

Length on Deck: 90′
Length Over All: 120′
Beam: 23′
Draft: 7′ (12′ centerboard down)
Displacement: 75 tons
Sail Area: 3500 sq. feet
Rig: bald-headed schooner
Power: yawl boat
Passengers: 24
Crew: 6

www.mainewindjammer.com

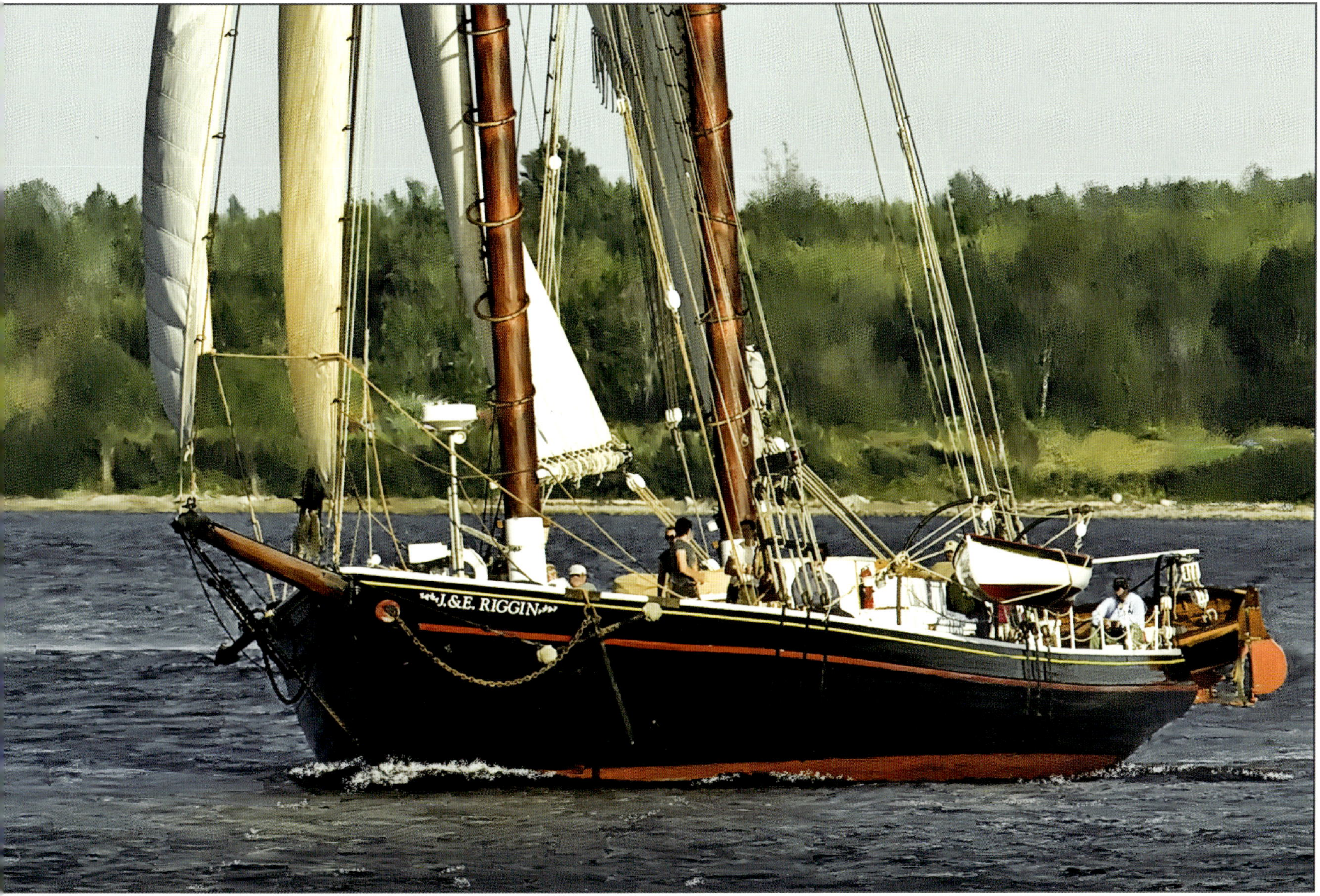
J.&E. RIGGIN

LEWIS R. FRENCH

The LEWIS R. FRENCH was launched in April of 1871 at Christmas Cove, Maine. Built by the French brothers and named for their father, she is the oldest commercial schooner in the United States and the last of thousands built in Maine during the 19th century. She freighted cargos of bricks, lumber, firewood, granite, fish, lime, supplies and Christmas trees. Totally rebuilt in 1971 for the Maine windjammer passenger trade, she has been designated a National Historic Landmark. Today she hails from Camden, Maine, and is owned and operated by Captain Garth Wells and Jenny Tobin.

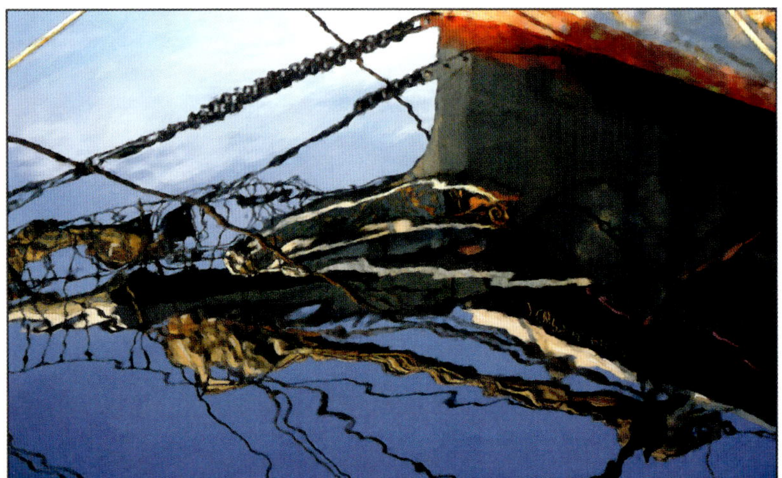

Length on Deck: 64′
Length Over All: 101′
Beam: 19′
Draft: 7′ 6″
Displacement: 56 tons
Sail Area: 2900 sq. feet
Rig: main topsail schooner
Power: yawl boat
Passengers: 23
Crew: 4

www.schoonerfrench.com

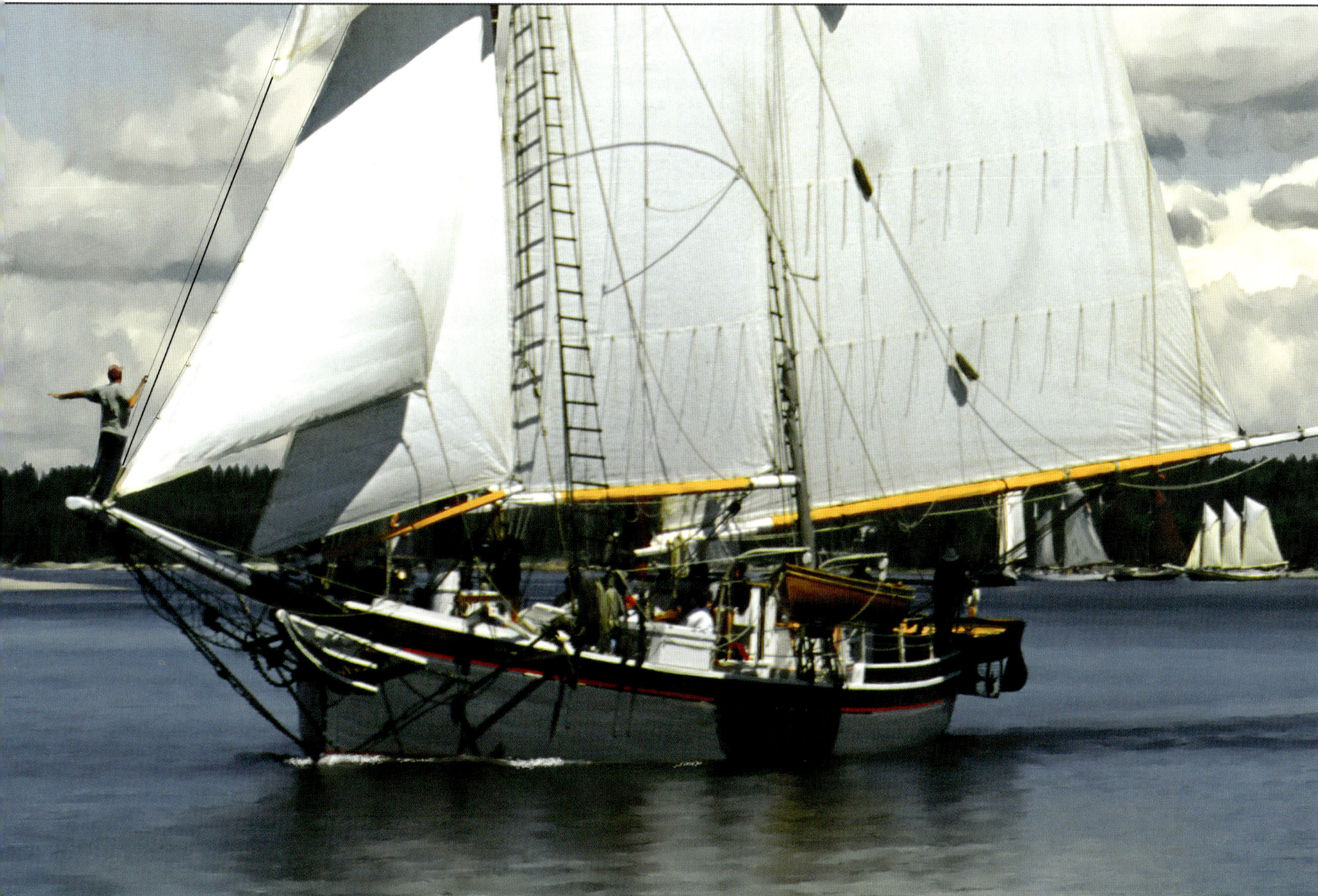

MARY DAY

The MARY DAY was built in 1962 by Harvey Gamage of South Bristol, Maine, for Captain Havilah Hawkins. She was the first vessel built specifically for the Maine windjammer passenger trade; also she is the only schooner with double topsail rig in the windjammer fleet. Today the MARY DAY is owned and operated by Captains Barry and Jennifer King and hails from Camden, Maine.

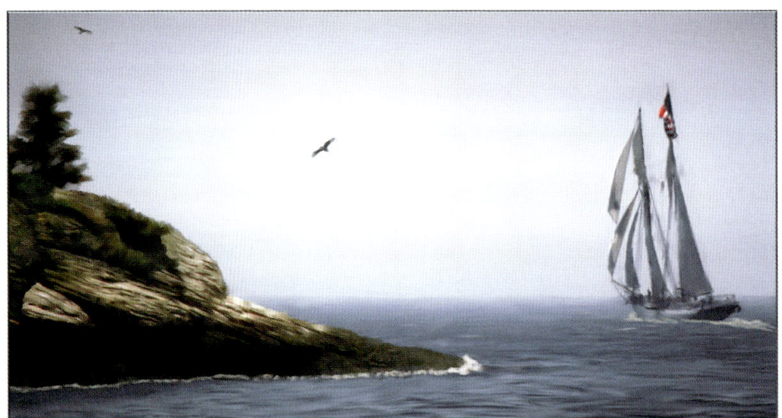

Length on Deck: 90′
Length Over All: 125′
Beam: 23′ 6″
Draft: 7′ (15′ centerboard down)
Displacement: 90 tons
Sail Area: 4500 sq. feet
Rig: topsail schooner
Power: yawl boat
Passengers: 28
Crew: 5

www.schoonermaryday.com

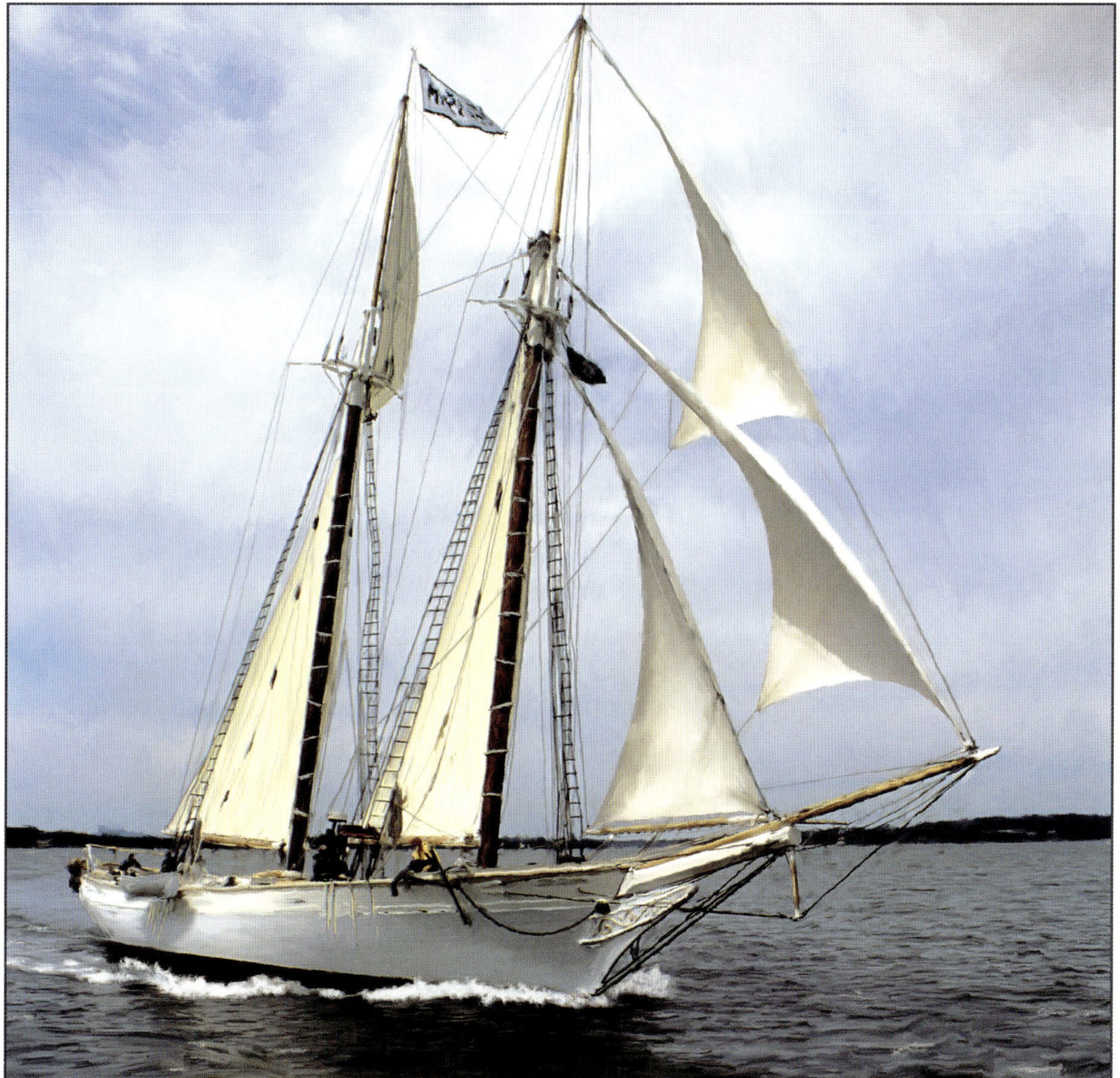

MERCANTILE

The MERCANTILE was built in 1916 by the Billings family of Deer Isle, Maine. A shoal-draft centerboarder, she transported barrel staves and firewood to the lime kilns along the Maine coast. She also carried cargoes of salt fish from Frenchboro and Swans Island, Maine to Gloucester, Massachusetts. A National Historic Landmark, today she is home-ported out of Camden, Maine, owned and operated by Captain Ray Williamson.

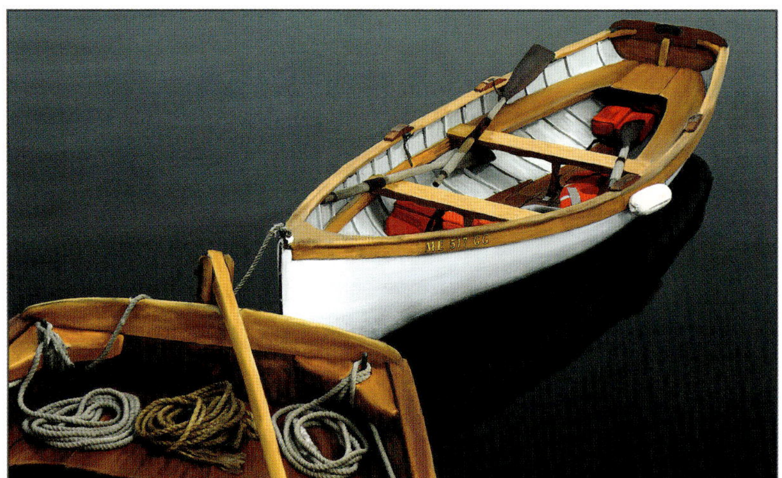

Length on Deck: 80′
Length Over All: 115′
Beam: 22′
Draft: 6′ 7″ (10′ 7″ centerboard down)
Displacement: 47 tons
Sail Area: 3015 sq. feet
Rig: bald-headed schooner
Power: yawl boat
Passengers: 29
Crew: 5

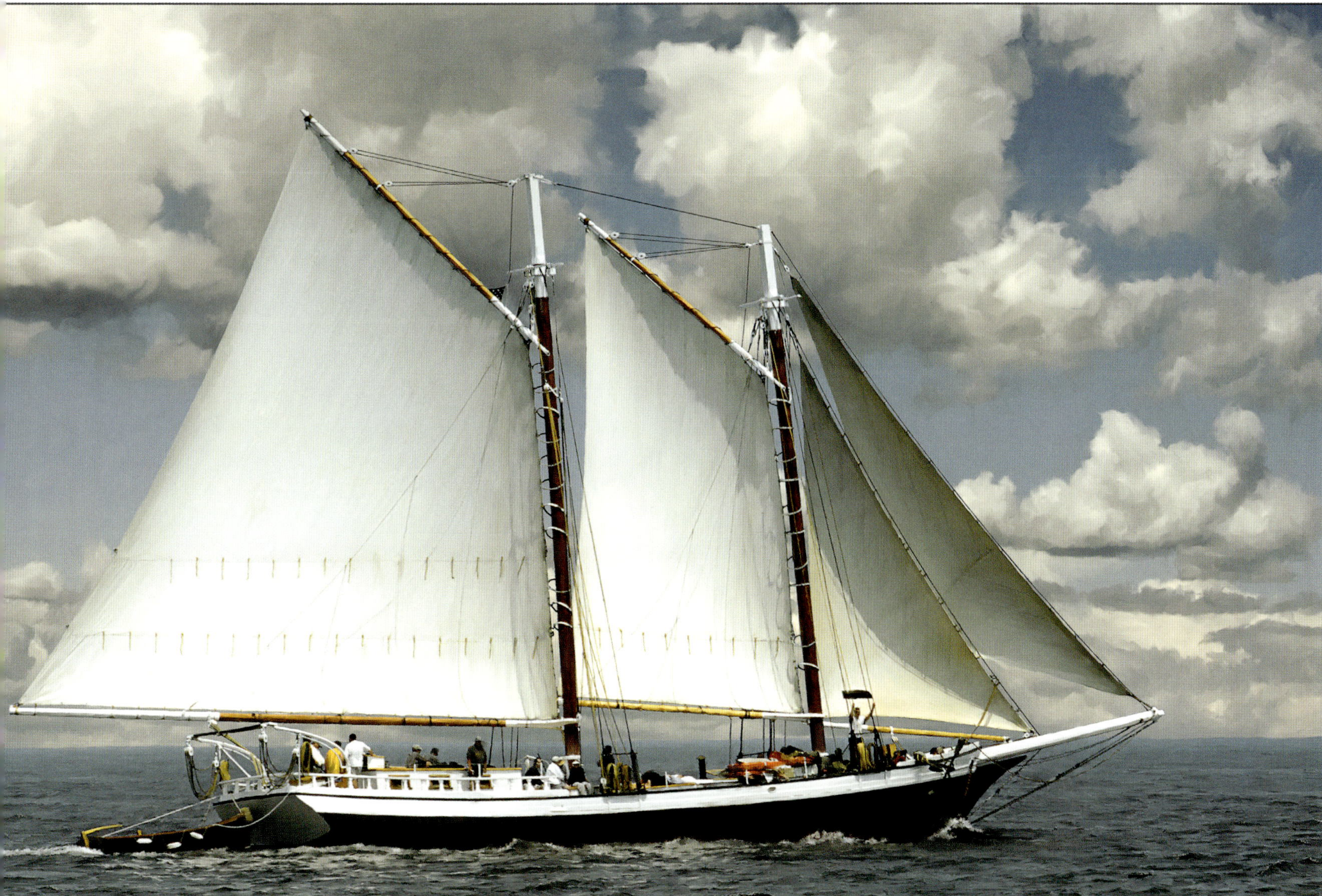

MISTRESS

MISTRESS combines the lines of an old coastal schooner with modern accommodations below decks, and an inboard engine. Built on Deer Isle, Maine, in 1960, she was later re-fitted for the Maine windjammer passenger trade. In 1992 she was rebuilt and lengthened by six feet. Today she is owned and operated by Captain Ray Williamson, out of Camden, Maine.

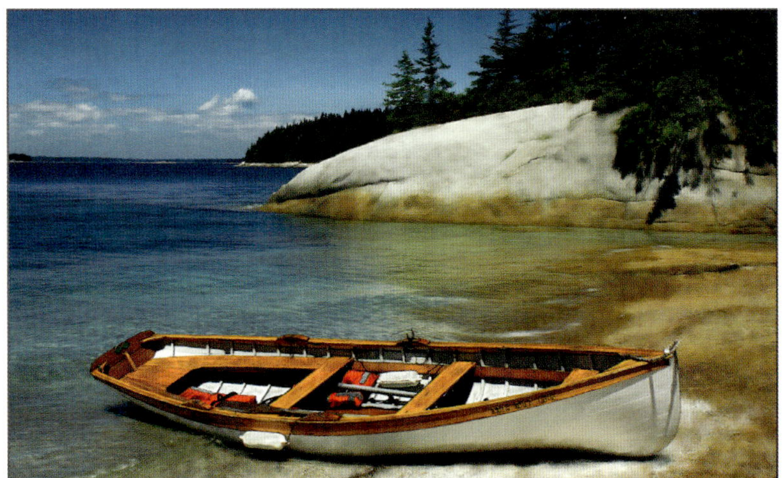

Length on Deck: 46′
Length Over All: 60′
Beam: 13′ 6″
Draft: 6′
Displacement: 13 tons
Sail Area: 1169 sq. feet
Rig: bald-headed schooner
Power: 60hp diesel
Passengers: 6
Crew: 2

www.mainewindjammercruises.com

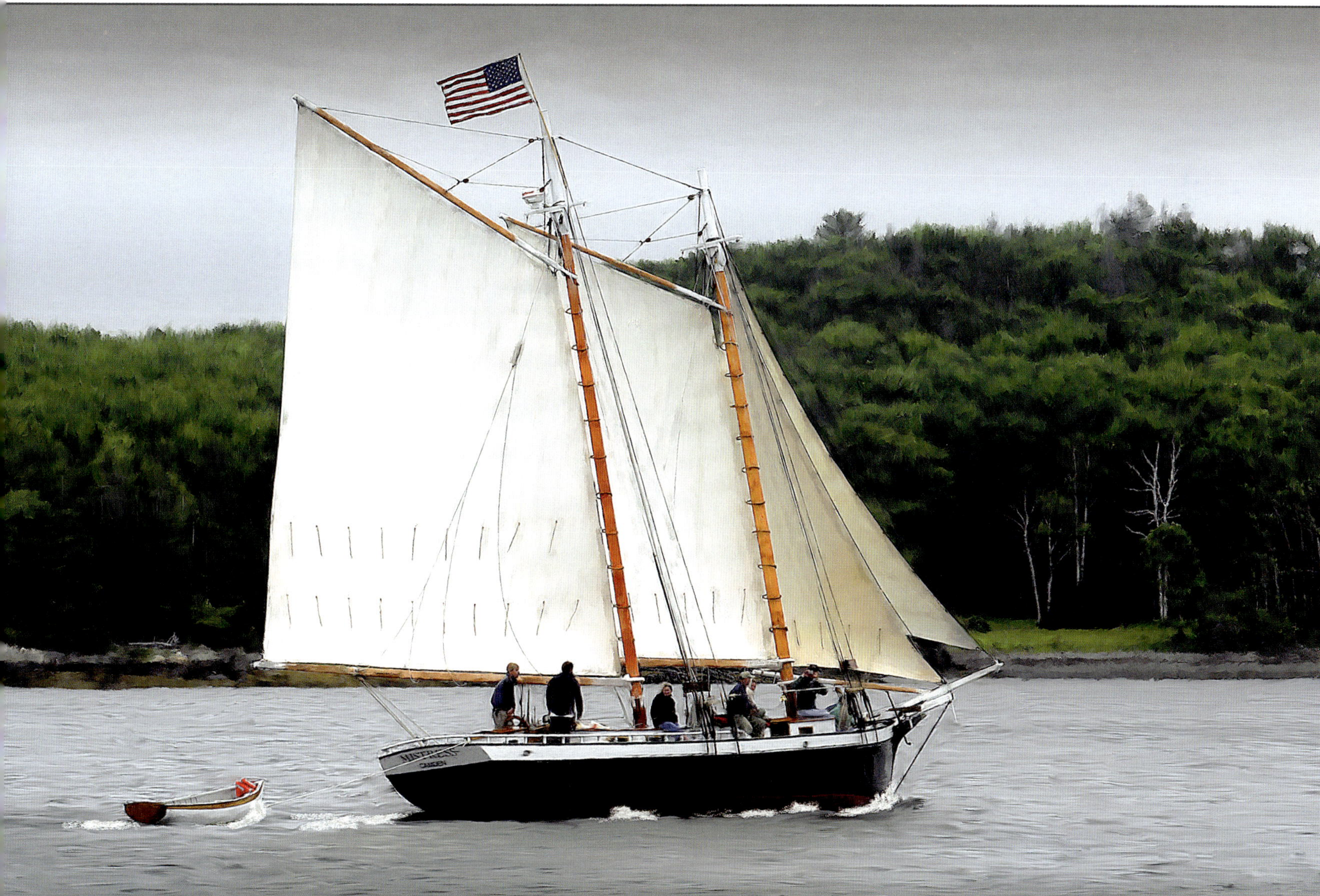

NATHANIEL BOWDITCH

Built in 1922 in East Boothbay, Maine, by the Hodgdon Brothers, the NATHANIEL BOWDITCH was designed by William Hand as a racing yacht, and in 1927 won the Bermuda Cup race. During World War II she was commissioned by the United States Coast Guard as an offshore German submarine search patrol vessel for New York harbor. After the war she was re-rigged as a commercial dragger for the fishing industry and sailed out of Stonington, Connecticut. In 1971 she was brought "Downeast", and completely rebuilt for the windjammer passenger trade. Today she is owned and operated by Captain Owen Dorr and hails from Rockland, Maine.

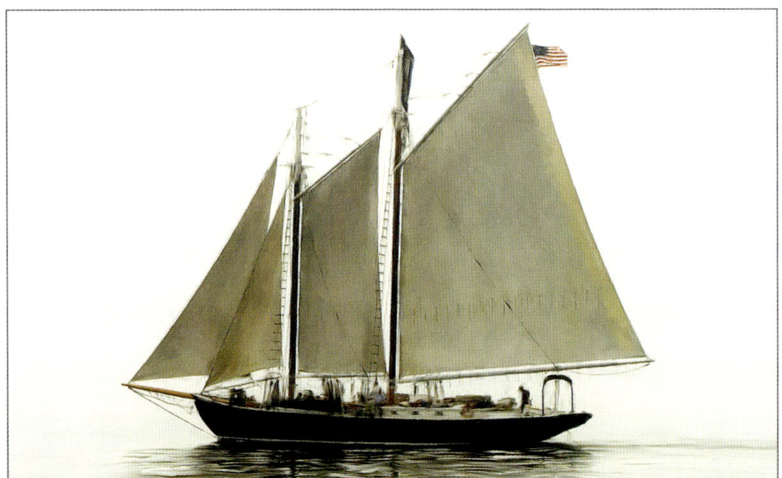

Length on Deck: 82′
Length Over All: 108′
Beam: 21′ 6″
Draft: 11′
Displacement: 150 tons
Sail Area: 3700 sq. feet
Rig: main topsail schooner
Power: Detroit diesel
Passengers: 24
Crew: 4

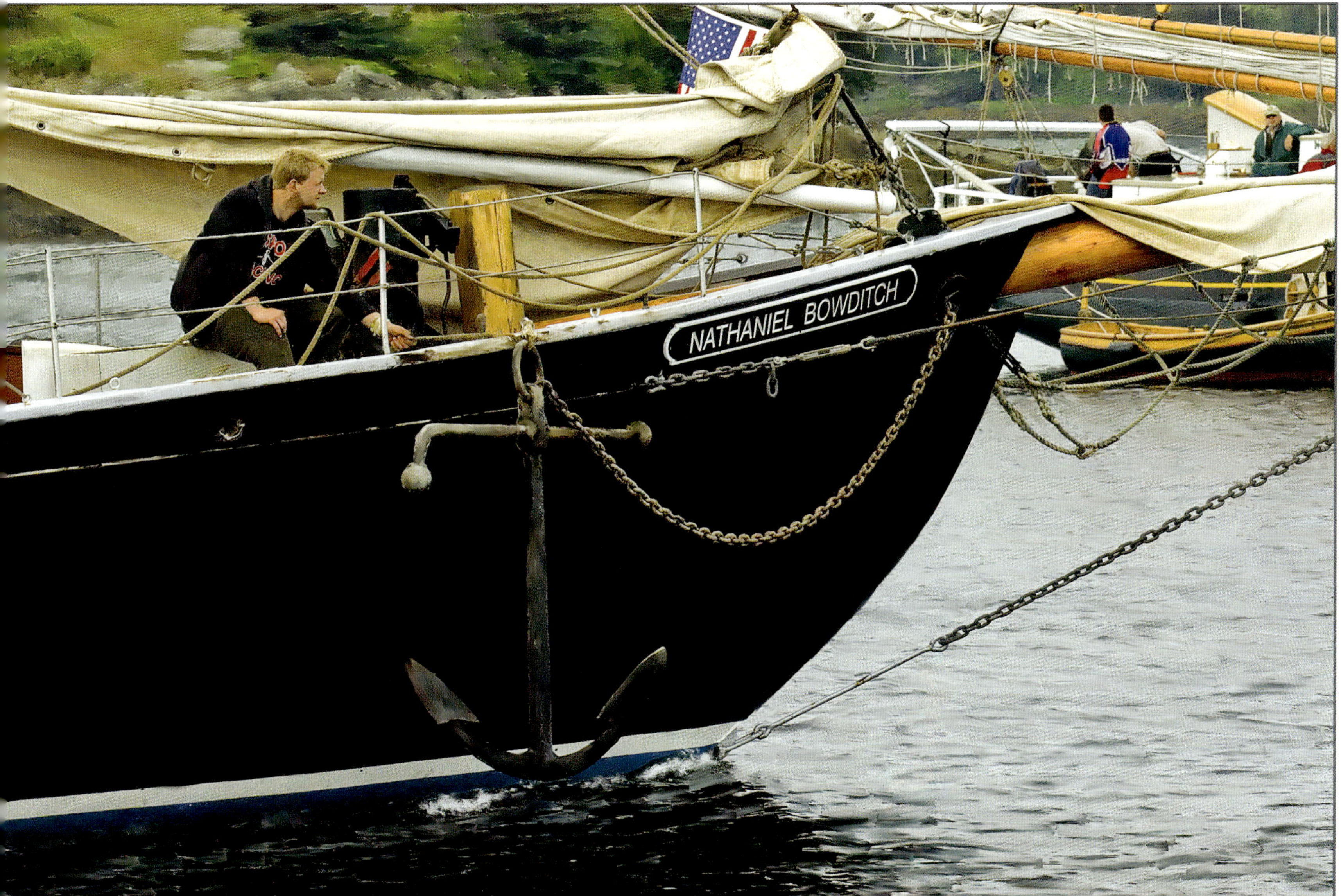
NATHANIEL BOWDITCH

STEPHEN TABER

The STEPHEN TABER was built in 1871 on Long Island, New York, to transport among other things, brick, coal, lumber, and oysters. From 1871 through 1920 she hauled freight around Long Island Sound and up the Hudson River. In 1936 she was brought "Downeast", rebuilt, and used to haul lumber on Penobscot Bay. In 1946 she was refitted for the Maine windjammer passenger trade. She has become known as the "good luck vessel" because of the caring attention she received from a series of owners through her many decades of service. The oldest documented sailing vessel in continuous service in the United States, she has been designated a National Historic Landmark. In 1980 she was purchased by Captain Ken Barnes, who sailed her in the Maine windjammer passenger trade for 25 years. Today his son, Captain Noah Barnes, sails her out of Rockland, Maine.

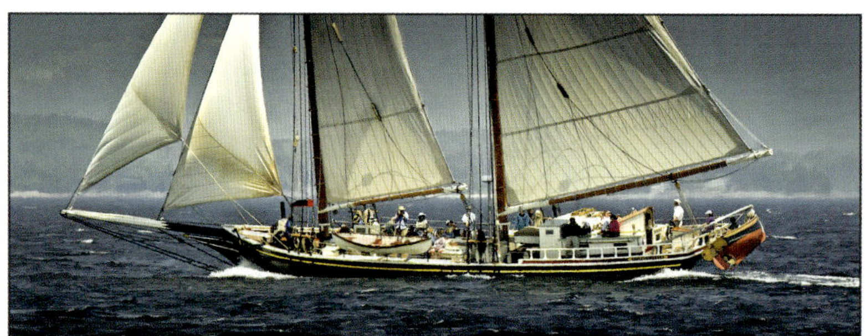

Length on Deck: 68′
Length Over All: 115′
Beam: 22′ 6″
Draft: 5′ (14′ 6″ centerboard down)
Sail Area: 3000 sq. feet
Rig: main topmast schooner
Power: yawl boat
Passengers: 22
Crew: 5

www.stephentaber.com

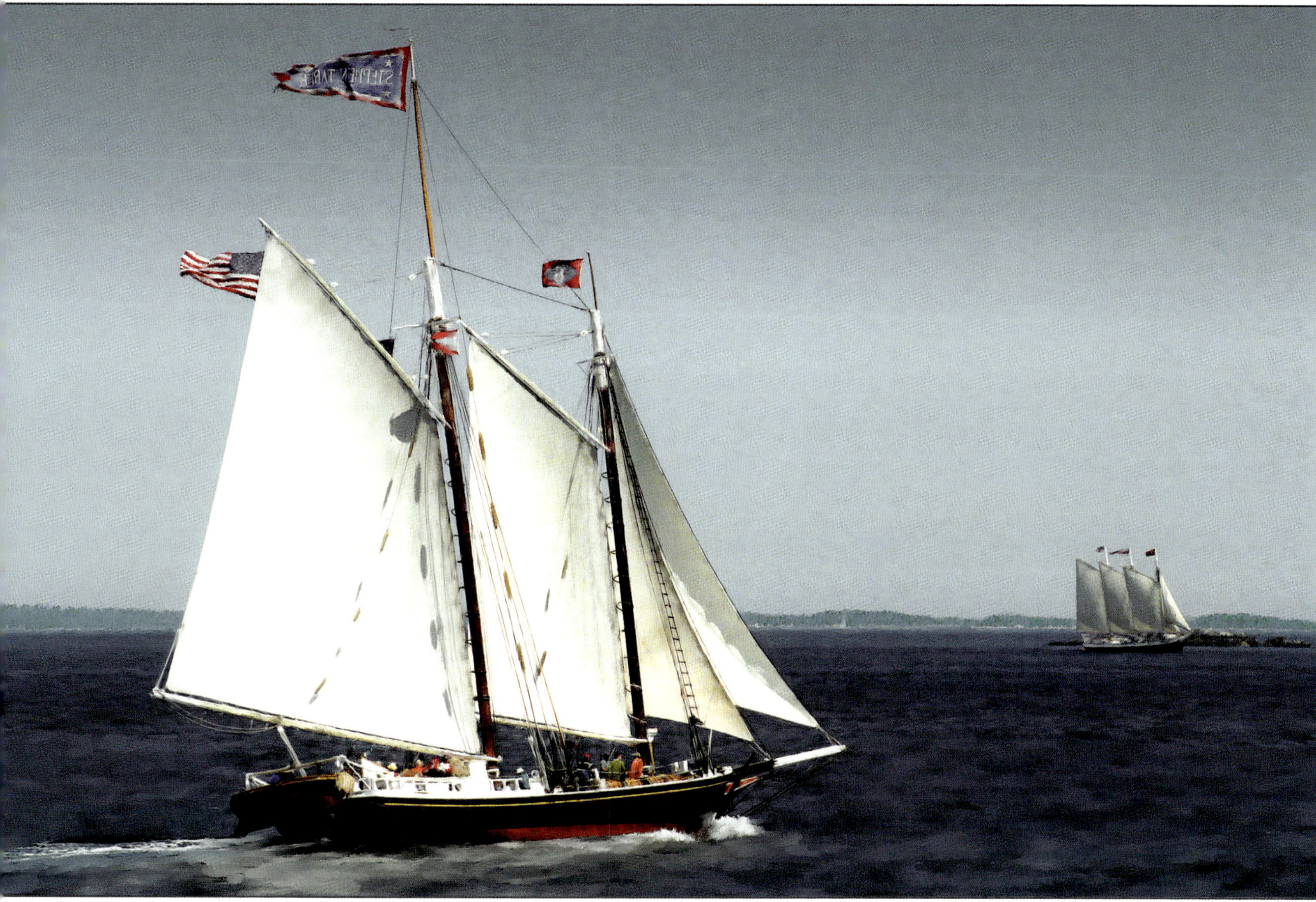

SUMMERTIME

SUMMERTIME was built in 1986 in Brooklin, Maine, by George Allen and Bill Brown, from locally-cut lumber. Her lines are of a Maine Pinky, circa 1830-1840, which the builders used from Howard Chapelle's book *American Fishing Schooners 1825-1935*, although the design predates the American Revolution. SUMMERTIME is owned and operated by Captain Bill Brown out of Brooklin, Maine.

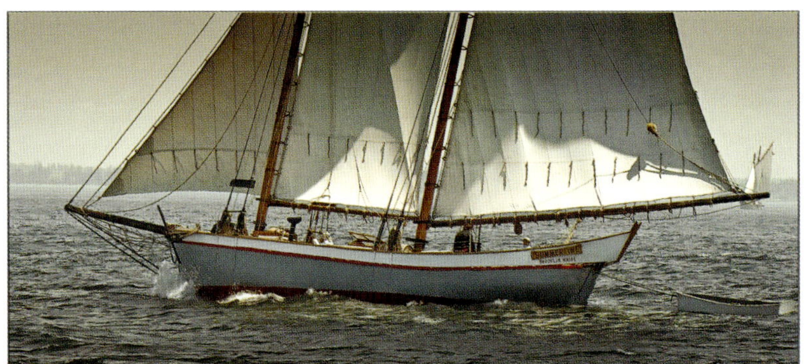

Length on Deck: 52′ 9″
Length Over All: 80
Beam: 13′ 7″
Draft: 7′ (12′ centerboard down)
Displacement: 37 tons
Sail Area: 1700 sq. feet
Rig: bald-headed schooner
Power: diesel engine
Passengers: 7
Crew: 3

www.schoonersummertime.com

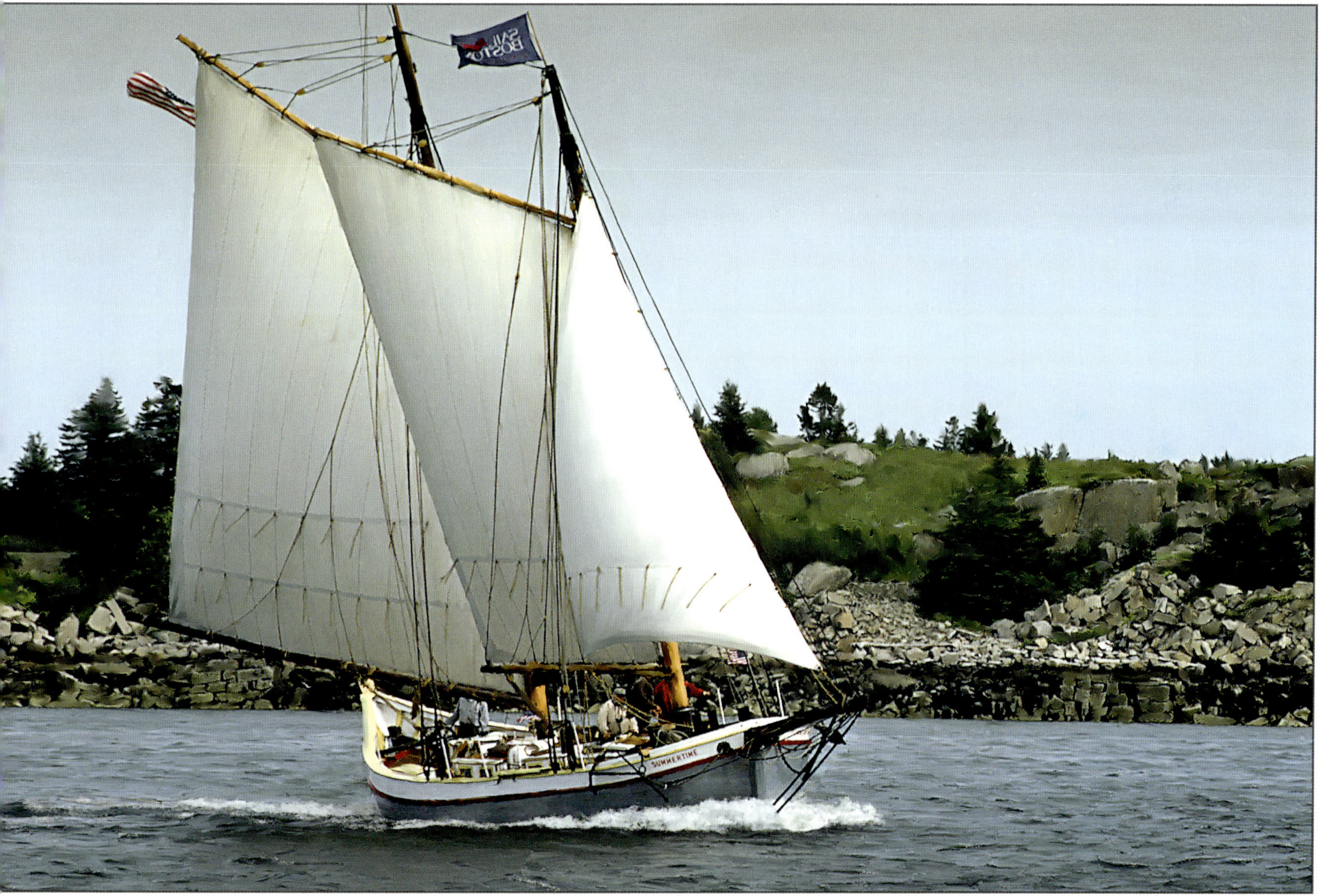
SUMMERTIME

TIMBERWIND

TIMBERWIND was built in 1931 at Union Wharf in Portland, Maine. Originally named PORTLAND PILOT, she earned her keep as the pilot boat for Portland Harbor, where she served until retirement in 1969. Rebuilt for the Maine passenger trade, she was renamed TIMBERWIND and today is owned and operated by Captain Bob Tassi, out of Rockport, Maine.

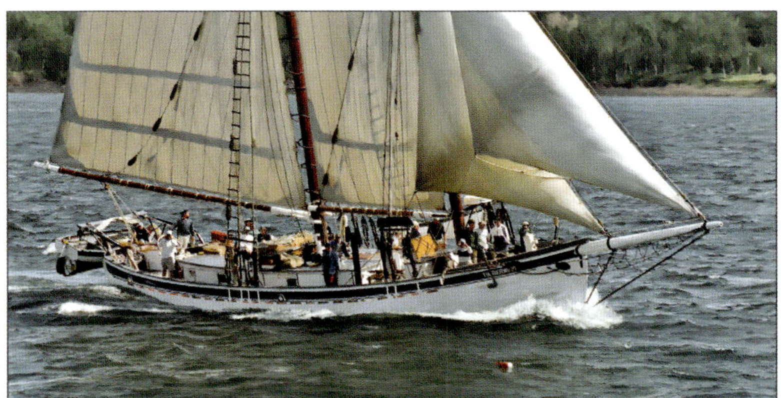

Length on Deck: 70′
Length Over All: 96′
Beam: 18′ 6′
Draft: 9′ 7″
Displacement: 85 tons
Sail Area: 2520 sq. feet
Rig: main topsail schooner
Power: yawl boat
Passengers: 20
Crew: 4

www.schoonertimberwind.com

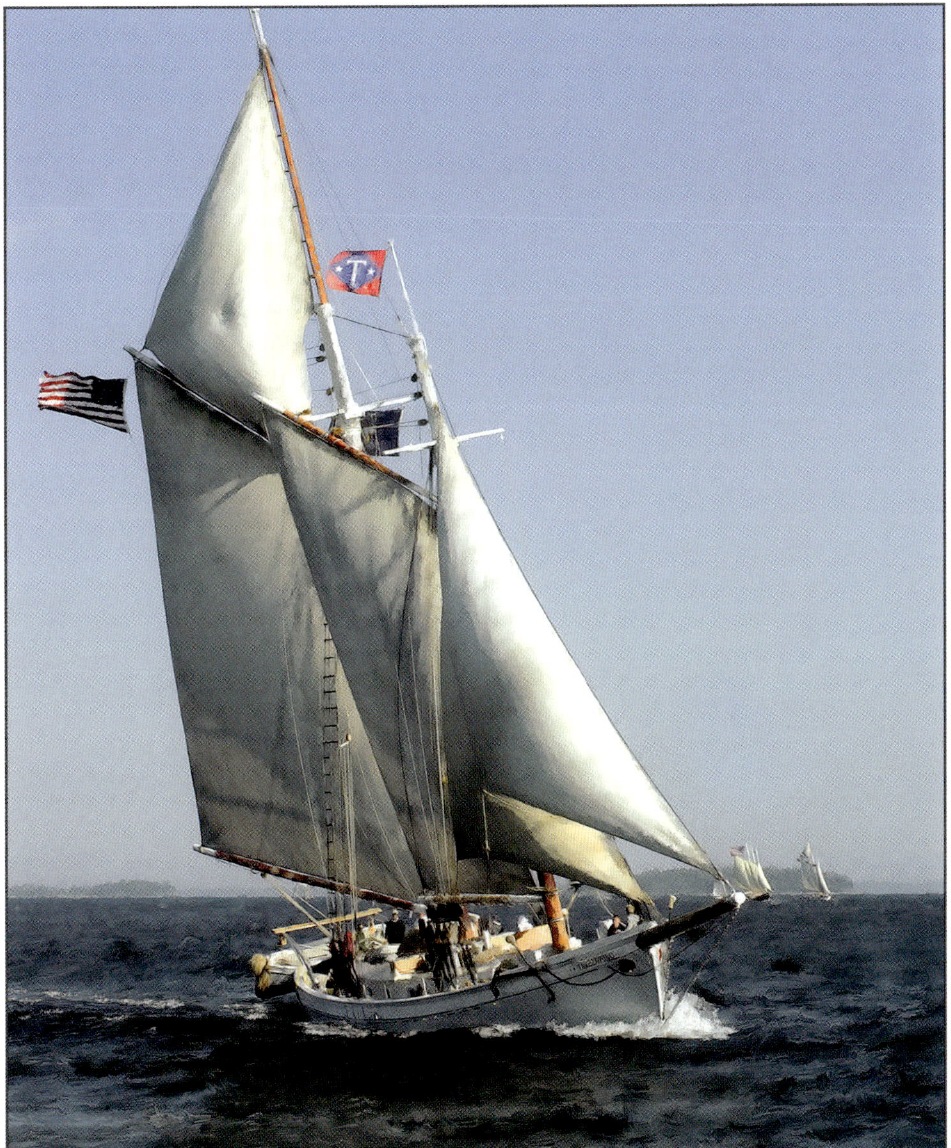

VICTORY CHIMES

VICTORY CHIMES was built in 1900 for Captain R.E. Riggin (related to the J.&E. RIGGIN family) and originally named EDWIN & MAUD. She was designed by George Phillips Company of Bethel, Delaware, to haul sawn lumber, grain, soft coal and fertilizer in and out of Chesapeake Bay. Purchased by Captain H.E. Knust in 1945 and converted for passenger trade, she sailed the Chesapeake Bay for nine years. She was then sold to the legendary Captain Frederick 'Boyd" Guild who renamed her VICTORY CHIMES and sailed her in the Maine windjammer fleet. More ownership changes resulted in a stint on the Great Lakes, before returning to Maine waters, where she now sails out of Rockland, Maine, under Captains Kip Files and Paul DeGaeta. In 1997 she was designated a National Historic Landmark.

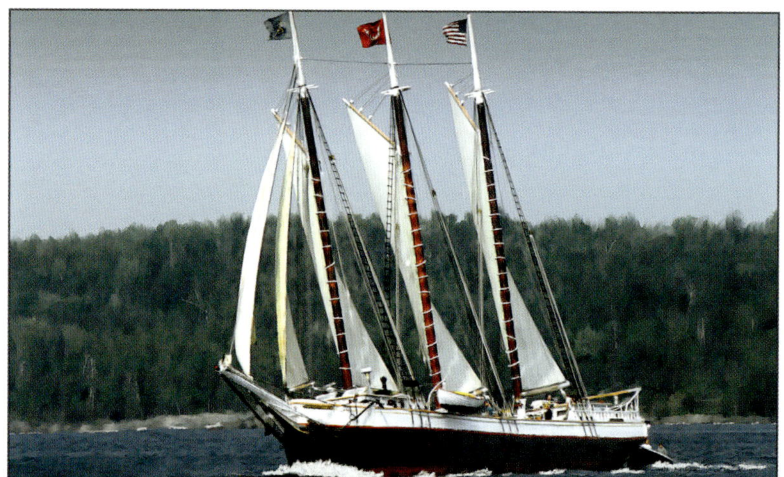

Length on Deck: 132′
Length Over All: 172′
Beam: 25′
Draft: 7′ 6″ (18′ centerboard down)
Displacement: 395 tons
Sail Area: 6500 sq. feet
Rig: bald-headed schooner
Power: yawl boat
Passengers: 44
Crew: 9

www.victorychimes.com

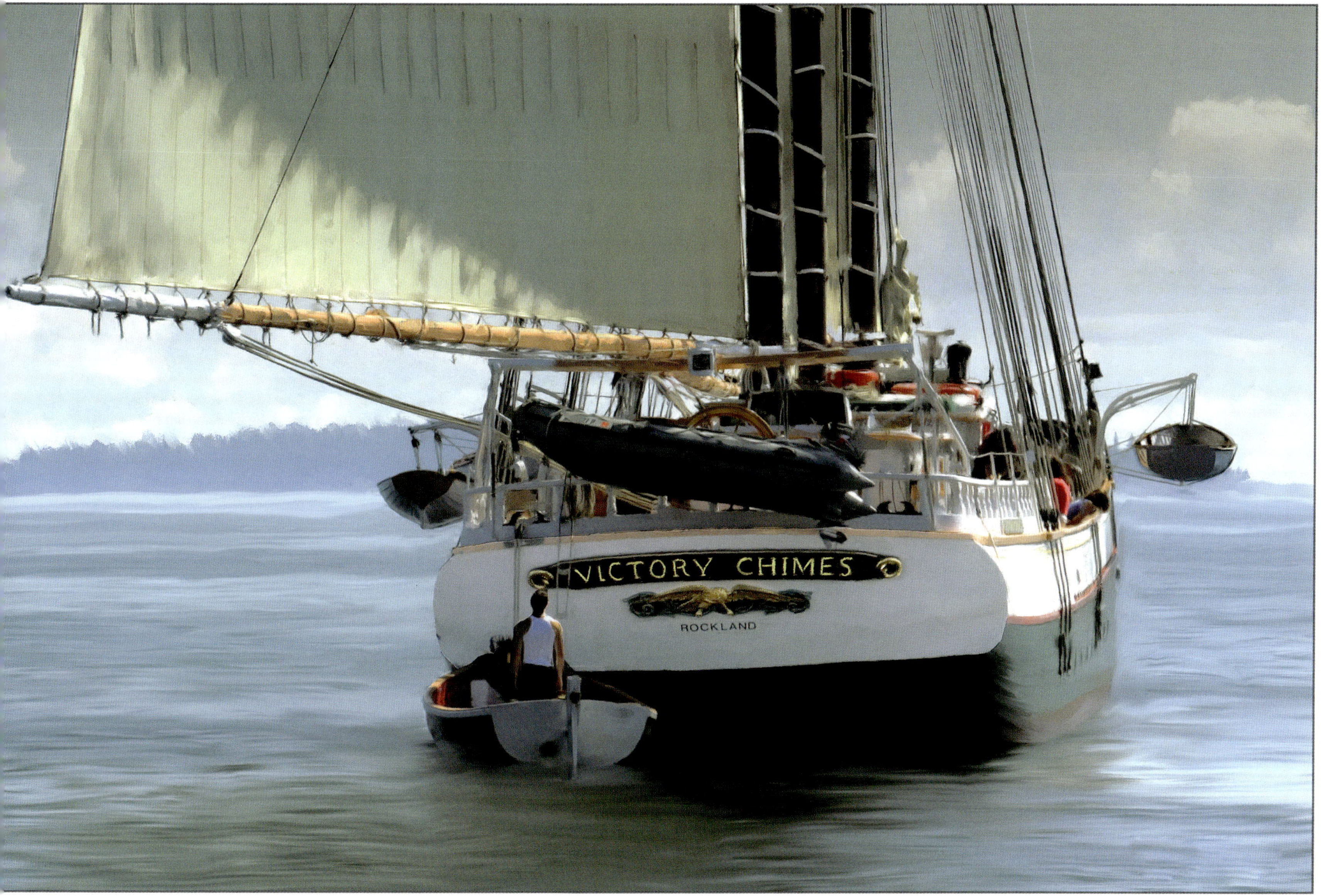
VICTORY CHIMES
ROCKLAND

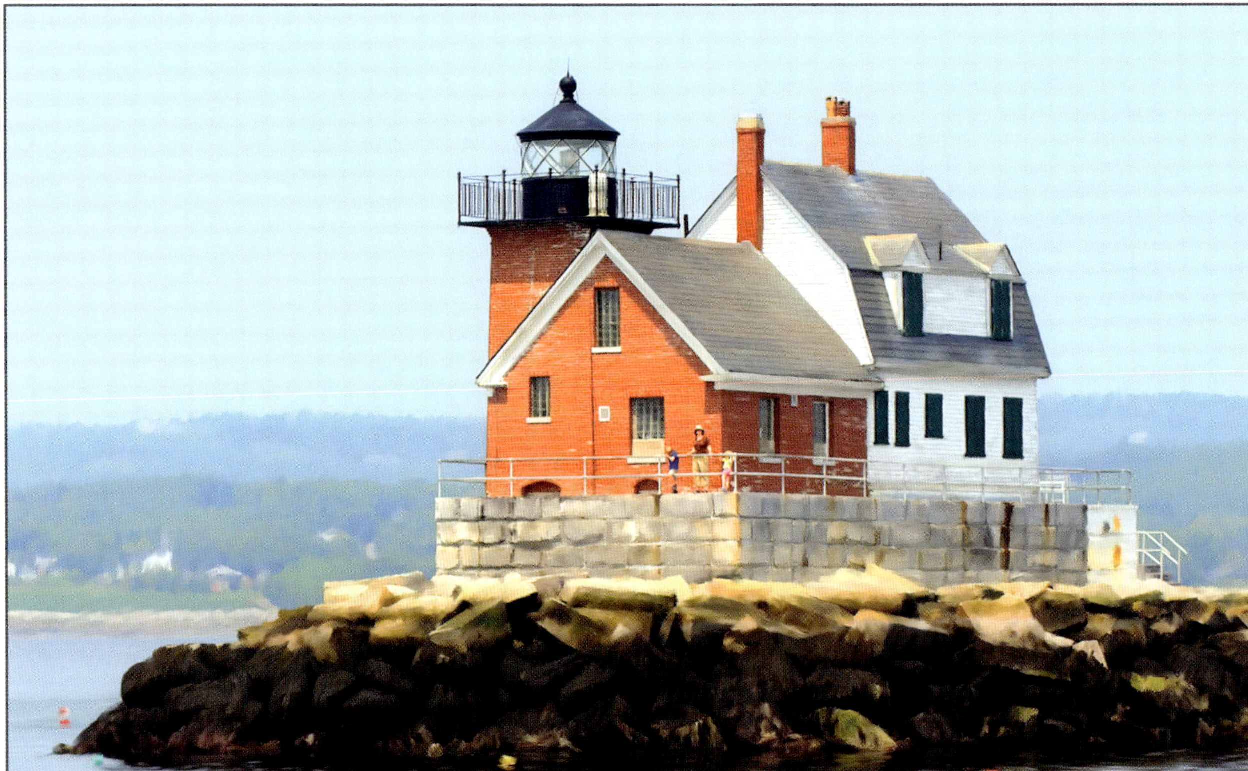

Rockland Breakwater Light

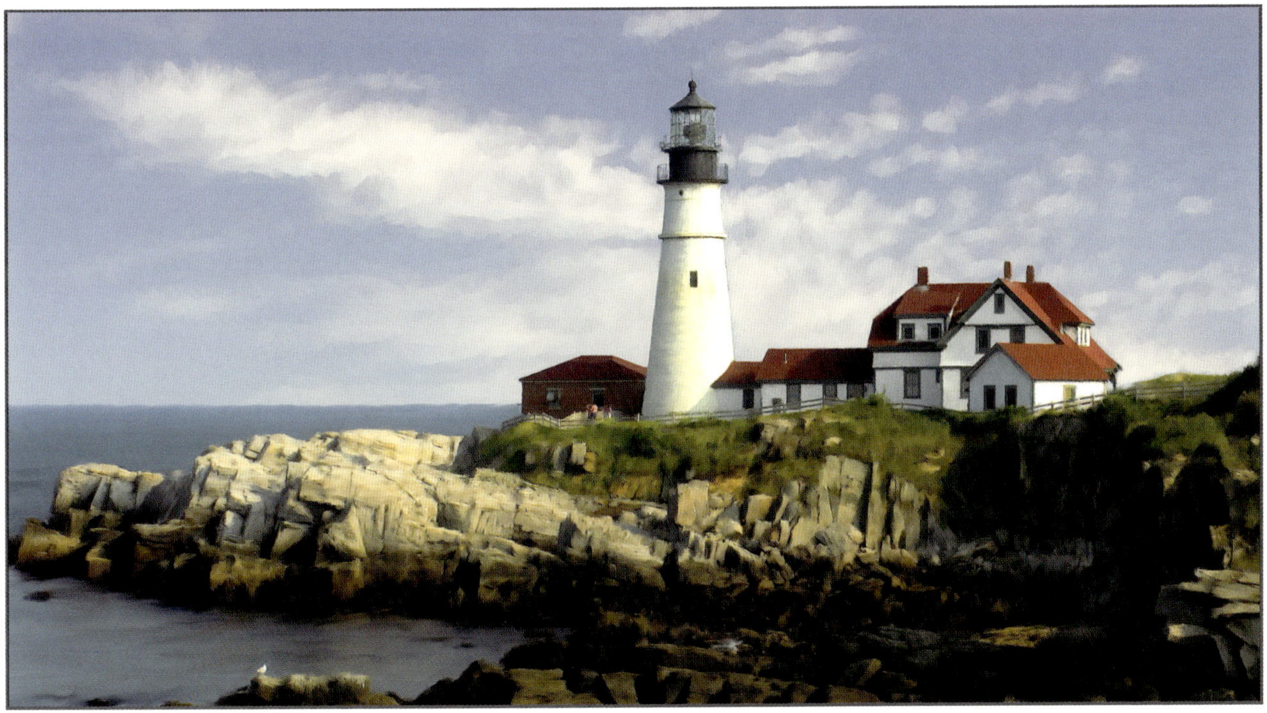

Portland Head Light

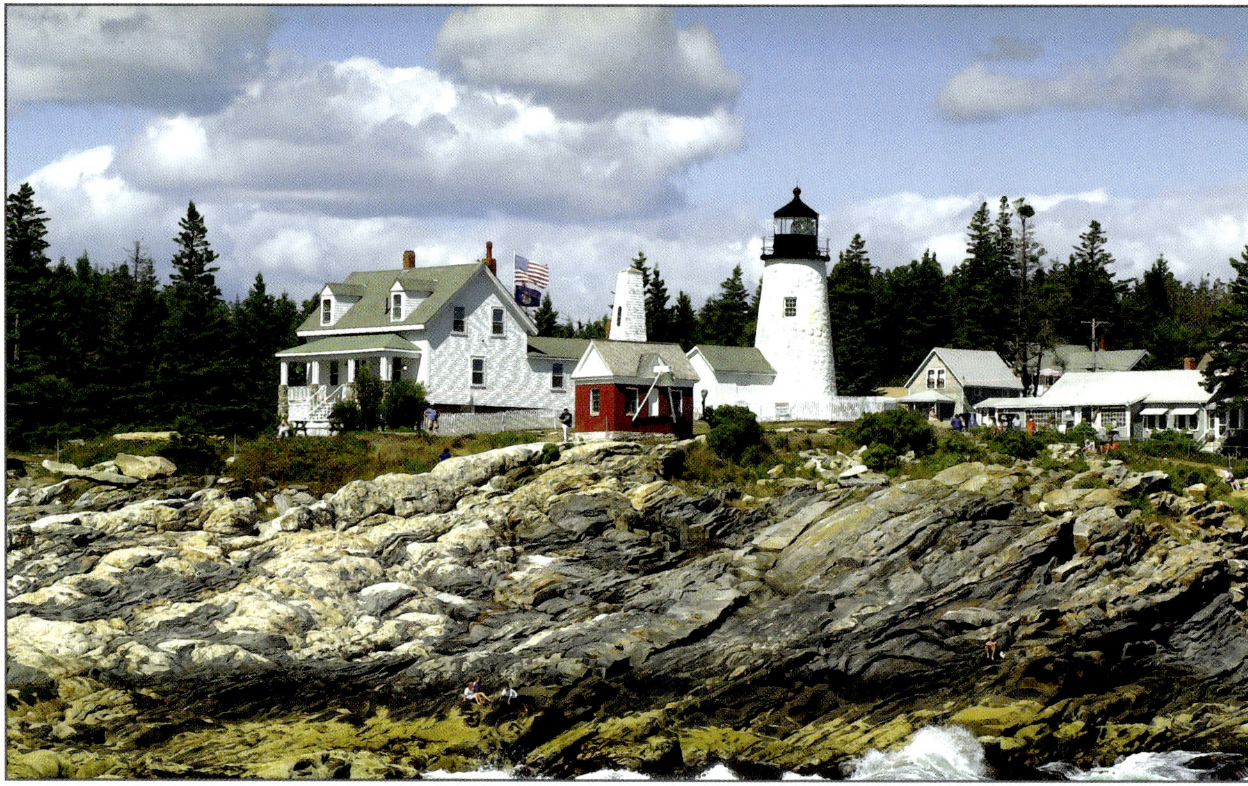

Pemaquid Light

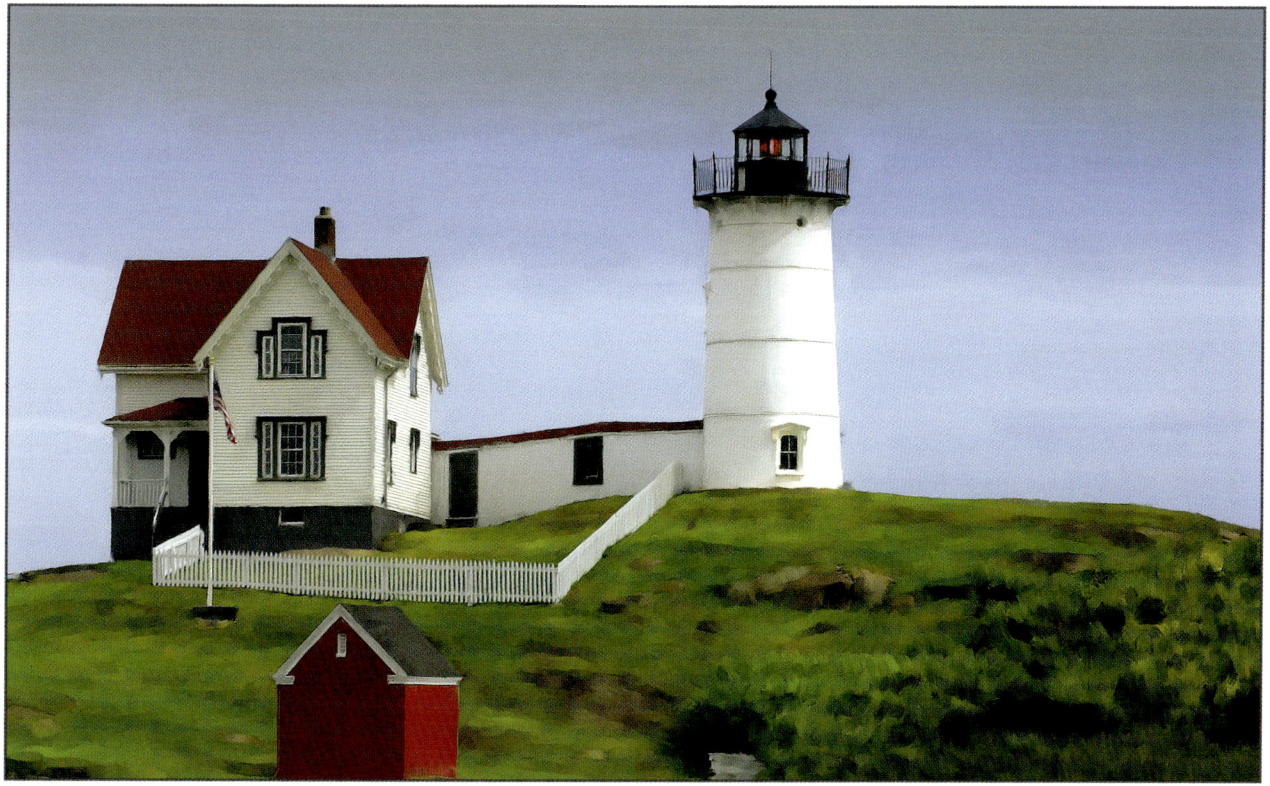

Cape Neddick "Nubble" Light